Double Exposure

Other Books by
Double Exposure

- Easy Songs for Your Singer Sewing Machine

- Drop the Canada Goose from the Endangered List
  and Other Droppings

- The Double Exposure Guide to Canola Harvesting

- The Rapper's Robert Service

- Innu Throat Singing for School Choirs

- How to Protect Yourself During a Laugh Riot

Double Exposure

Linda Cullen
& Bob Robertson

WHITECAP BOOKS
Vancouver / Toronto

Edited by Pat Crowe
Cover design by Steve Penner
Cover photograph by Kent Kallberg
Interior design by Rose Cowles

Printed and bound in Canada.

Canadian Cataloguing in Publication Data

Cullen, Linda
 Double exposure

ISBN 1-55110-379-6

 1. Canadian wit and humor (English). I. Robertson, Bob.
II. Title.
PS8555.U44D68 1995   C818'.540208   C95-910689-9
PR9199.3.C84D68 1995

Dedicated . . .

To whom it may concern

Table of Contents

CHAPTER 5.

Identity Crisis! Am I Canadian Because I Drink Beer, or Am I Drinking Beer Because My UI Cheque Just Arrived?

CHAPTER 6.

Canada's Unsolved Mysteries

🦶 While sitting in the House of Commons, Sheila Copps removes her shoes and sticks her feet in a tub of tapioca pudding, saying it relaxes her feet, keeps her mind focused, and is handy if she feels like having a snack.

How To Use This Book

Now that you are the proud owner of *Double Exposure*, it is very important to know how to use it. Almost every day, in every city in the country, there are thousands, possibly millions, of people who purchase books, and then use them in completely inappropriate ways. How many times have you seen somebody reading Margaret Atwood's *The Handmaid's Tale* on the bus on the way to work? This would be considered inappropriate book usage. The depressing nature of the story can have a serious negative effect on productivity. Studies have shown that the poor attitude of most public servants has been directly connected to reading *The Handmaid's Tale* before punching in.

There are many acceptable ways to use this book. For example, reading portions of it aloud at parties is an excellent application. You will then be thought of as an individual who knows how to recognize humour when you see it, and no doubt will improve what is probably a fairly dull gathering, especially if the hosts are about to show videos of the births of all their children, or someone suggests playing Trivial Pursuit—Mensa Edition. If you choose to read this book while driving, also a very acceptable usage, be sure to keep your window rolled down, because you will almost certainly want to yell out your favourite parts to the car on your left, including, of course, the title of the book. If you have a sunroof, keep that open, too. Bus drivers and truckers can always use a good laugh, plus it will take their attention off that unsightly bald spot. Reading in the relative comfort of the "privy" is an age-old tradition. However, we suggest you restrict enjoyment of the *Double Exposure* book to your own household lavatory, because co-workers have been known to become very suspicious of anyone who appears to be having an overabundance of pleasure during the call of nature.

After extensive research, we have concluded that the best way to use the book is to grasp it tightly in both hands while listening to *Double Exposure* on CBC Radio every Saturday morning at 11:30. If you follow these recommendations carefully, you will benefit from MCO (Maximum Comedy Output). However, we cannot be held responsible for any unforeseen consequences that may occur should these guidelines be ignored.

Stan (Tom) McFrugal
Publisher

Congratulations!

You are now the proud owner of *Double Exposure*. Whether you purchased this book yourself or received it as a gift, there is no doubt it will have a profound impact on your life. There have been great success stories about people who have read and utilized the book. Many have become more confident and more secure with themselves. They have experienced cosmic oneness with their tantric past-life Zen master and roller blade trainers, and their inner children have grown up and moved out. Mr. Nigel Mealy, a door-to-door door salesman, states that before he read *Double Exposure*, business had been difficult, to say the least. "The problem was," says Mr. Mealy, "practically every home I went up to already had a door, sometimes two or three." Then, Mr. Mealy picked up a copy of the book. The change was remarkable! "The change," says Mr. Mealy, "to quote an old expression, was remarkable! I was selling doors like they were hotcakes, and then I started selling hotcakes like they were doors. My income went from $582 a year to $675,000 a year. Thank goodness for *Double Exposure*!"

Mrs. Myrtle Dorking said she used to spend $500 a month calling the Psychic Network for the answers to her problems, but, after just one week with *Double Exposure*, "I don't have to phone the Psychic Network any more. I simply place my hands on the book, and I can instantly predict my own future. I can also predict the arrival times of all Via Rail trains across the country, plus or minus six hours," says Mrs. Dorking enthusiastically. "It even stimulated hair growth on my husband, Dick Dorking. Of course, he wasn't bald, so children tend to stare, but, all in all, I think it's worth it."

Will this book change your life? Absolutely. Just by holding it in your hands, you will instantly become more attractive to people, because now everyone will know what excellent taste you have in reading material. That is the incredible power of *Double Exposure*.

"And by night I put on dis hat and become 'Pea-Souperman'!"

The number of socialists in Canada has drastically decreased,
due mostly to confused mating habits.

Political Hinterland
— WHO'S WHO —

As another winter descends across the vast Canadian lands, the creatures of the political hinterland have not been idle. On Canada's easternmost shores, called simply "The Rock," the Cly dwells on its hard times. The Cly's once abundant food supply is now filling the bellies of its Spanish enemies, and it begins to eye, hungrily, the harbour seals off its coast. The Cly dwells also on the suffering it has endured over the past seasons. First, all the cucumbers died, then the cod disappeared, and now it has exerted itself so much looking for oil that it has given itself a Hibernia. Another Rock dweller, the Briney Tobin, recognized by its swelled head, has vacated the empty Turbot grounds, and has been salmoned to the western shores. Meanwhile, across the turbulent Cabot Strait, near the Bedford Basin, a Savage attack continues on the leader of the Bluenose flock. This Welsh Warbler may soon become extinct. Nearby, on the green gabled island of Anne, the loopy Call of the Beck can be heard, its territory unsettled recently by a flock of large cranes, forerunners of the amphibious, strait-hopping Flink. Across the Bay of Fundy, the Barrel-chested McKenna with its nasally corporate cry of "Tax Break! Tax Break!" continues to lure curious courier pigeons from far away, as it pecks away at the CoR.

As winter blows in across the St. Lawrence, the creatures of the eastern townships have cause to gaspe! The Great Puffing Parizeau, a stupid creature, has not attracted enough of its kind to fly the coop with its droning "Ummm" calls. Its cousin the Bloc Flocker, leader of the Bloc Flock, seems bent on irritating the Puffing Parizeau, which hopes to see the Bloc Flock off. In the depression north of Lake Ontario, the Bobrae has now been driven into the rough by the Great Blue Harris with its screech of "Fore! Years." The Bobrae, without its longtime ally, the Bobwhite, simply went in circles due to an uncontrollable left wing.

Further west, where the Red River meets the Assiniboine, the Twogarries still rule the roost in this land of gambolling animals. Next door on the bald prairie, the Royal Roamingnose, fresh from another fight, remains the cock, and unruffled.

The Royal Roamingnose has badly depleted the Haver stock, and almost eliminated the once high-flying Jail Boyds. Where the foothills meet the Rockies, the Ponderosa Klein, never an early bird, has proved to be more bull than expected. Despite its slashing and cutting style, it continues to perch high on poles, while still feeding off nearby fields of barley and hops. On the Pacific shores, the Bald-headed Mikey continues to plummet, as it lives up to its Latin name, *Bonehead Grandeflora*.

And, where the Rideau meets the Ottawa River, the One-sided Cretin, or, in Latin, *Littleguyus Shawiniganus*, still mocks the Red-faced Tories, now, alas, reduced to a single breeding pair. In their place, the strident cries of the Muddleheaded Manning, or *Prestonius Taxrevolticus* have taken over that part of the hill. And that's "Political Hinterland Who's Who."

REFORM PARTY OF CANADA

"I was sure I told them the **Ottawa** Convention Centre.
Maybe they all went to Oshawa."

Our Favourite

FRONT PAGE  CHALLENGE

"Okay, panel, you've got two minutes to guess our hidden challenger. Pierre?"

"Did it happen on a continent beginning with 'Z'?"

"No, Pierre. No continents begin with 'Z'."

"I must have been thinking of Zimbabwe. Is it the new Zimbabwe flag?"

"Sorry, Pierre. You're way off the mark."

"I smell saffron! It's Mahatma Ghandi, isn't it?"

"No, Pierre. Betty?"

"This isn't the sex change man, Jorgensen?"

"Good guess, Betty, but, here's a hint, we're looking for more 'eyes' than that."

"More than that. Five! It's the Dionne Quintuplets!"

"Wrong, Betty. I may have thrown you off earlier when I mentioned robes to Pierre. Jack?"

"It's Robespierre, the French revolutionary!"

"He's dead, Jack."

"He's dead? Is that the story, then? Robespierre dead! No? Alright then, he's very ill."

"No, panel, it's more recent than the French revolution. Allan?"

"This wouldn't be about mini-skirts from the '60s?"

"Well, Allan, you're on the right track. Think of dirt."

While sitting on the *Front Page Challenge* panel, Pierre Berton would write his many books on a typewriter hidden under the desk, using only his feet.

"Dirt. Is this Xaviera Hollander, the Happy Hooker? God, I hope so!"

"No, panel, you're all wrong. Our challenger is none other than "Stompin' Tom Connors.""

"Och! The hockey player!"

"And the story is, he's got a new record out called *Goober the Tuber*."

"I still smell saffron!"

(Thunderous applause at this point.)

Audience reacts to cancellation of *Front Page Challenge*.

"Look at dis! I am an honourary doctor. Does dis mean I can start honourary extra billing?"

Fisheries Minister Brian Tobin (right) displays illegal net used by Spanish ice fishermen.

THE DOUBLE EXPOSURE CANCON

1. **Atom Egoyan is:**
   (a) a famous film director
   (b) the first Japanese nuclear test
   (c) uncle of Atom Ant

2. **Carol Shields won the Pulitzer Prize for writing:**
   (a) *The Stone Diaries*
   (b) *The Stones of Madison County*
   (c) "Meet the Flintstones"

3. **Bruno Gerussi is best known for:**
   (a) *The Beachcombers*
   (b) beating Whipper Billy Watson
   (c) writing his autobiography, *Gerussi Park*

4. **The *Edmund Fitzgerald* sank because:**
   (a) of a bad storm
   (b) it was overloaded with Gordon Lightfoot CDs and cassettes
   (c) it struck the *Ella Fitzgerald*

5. **The people who write *Double Exposure* are on:**
   (a) CBC Radio, Saturdays at 11:30 a.m.
   (b) antidepressants
   (c) a humus-rich diet

6. **Roch Voisine is:**
   (a) an Acadian pop star
   (b) an eye-wash used by guitar players
   (c) French for "Rolling Stones"

7. **Alan Thicke got his name because of:**
   (a) his parents
   (b) his I.Q.
   (c) he didn't like his real name, Alan Idiot

8. **The Toronto Symphony Orchestra's conductor is:**
   (a) Jukka-Pekka Saraste
   (b) Jyrki Lumme
   (c) Polski Ogorki

9. ***The Road to Avonlea* is about:**
   (a) people on Prince Edward Island
   (b) sixty minutes long
   (c) Canada's first Avon lady

10. **The Guess Who were:**
    (a) Winnipeg musicians
    (b) Sidney Poitier and Katharine Hepburn
    (c) Joe Clark's government

11. **The CRTC was created so that:**

    (a) Canadian content would be broadcast

    (b) Keith Spicer wouldn't have to be put in a home

    (c) Bobby Curtola would be heard forever

12. **David Letterman's band leader is:**

    (a) Paul Shaffer

    (b) Schick Shaver

    (c) Sheb Wooley

13. **Canada's Marshall McLuhan said:**

    (a) "The medium is the message."

    (b) "I like my steak medium."

    (c) "You look after Miss Kitty, Festus, I'll get the bad guys."

14. **Dini Petty is:**

    (a) a TV talk show host

    (b) a small-minded dinosaur

    (c) a form of necking in Dini, Saskatchewan

15. **Leonard Cohen's music has immortalized:**

    (a) the beauty of Montreal

    (b) the dreariness of the long distance musician

    (c) the monetary potential of droning

16. **Don Messer's TV program was called a "Jubilee" because:**

    (a) it celebrated east coast music

    (b) it was officially opened by King George V

    (c) most of the sets were made with flaming cherries

17. **"Mr. Black" is listed as one of Canada's richest men. He is:**

    (a) newspaper magnate Conrad Black

    (b) CBC Radio host Arthur Black

    (c) Black and White Cabs co-owner Sidney Black

18. **k.d. lang absolutely refuses to:**

    (a) eat meat

    (b) do something with her hair

    (c) perform duets with Julio Iglesias

19. **The Crash Test Dummies are:**

    (a) a successful pop group

    (b) the people who wrote *Dumb and Dumber*

    (c) the parliamentary committee on gun control

20. **Most Canadians don't know:**

    (a) all the words to "O Canada"

    (b) how to spell Ralph Benmergui

    (c) why Valerie Pringle is so darned happy

From Parliament

PRIVATE MEMBERS' BILLS THAT WERE NEVER PASSED

Member: Alphonso Pyromanica (Lib.)
Riding: Brome-Isseltzer
Bill C-874–"Fireplace Registration"

Whereas: all fireplaces are inherently dangerous, having given thousands of Canadians nasty burns, as well as teary, stinging eyes if the flue is not open when it is lit, and, whereas according to police records, said fireplaces have been used in a large number of robberies in Canada, most recently a convenience store in Mississauga where two masked men ran into the store after midnight and demanded all the cash in the safe, "Or else, we'll try and start a fire in this fireplace with these Presto Logs"; be it resolved that the Parliament of Canada requires all Canadians to register their fireplaces in a National Fireplace Registry, regardless of whether the fireplaces are used for hunting purposes, knowing full well that in the fall many hunters head for their local woods to hunt animals by attracting them to a cozy, well-lit fireplace, or just by collectors who mount and frame their fireplaces on the walls of their homes; and keeping in mind that even though "Fires Don't Burn, People Do," nevertheless, to reduce the number of accidental deaths by fireplace we hereby recommend passage of this Bill C-874–"Fireplace Registration."

Canada's newest frigate, HMCS *Come-By-Chance,* on anti-submarine patrol.

Name which one is the (a) father of many Canadians (b) owner of a failed french fry machine (c) driver of the getaway car, and (d) Snagglepuss impersonator.

 John Turner is famous for patting Iona Campagnola on the behind with his hand, although he was more fond of taking off his shoes in the House, and throwing them at MPs' heads when they weren't looking.

A Pound of That Music, Please!

PRESS RELEASE FROM WEIGHTS AND MEASURES CANADA, NOVEMBER 1ST, 1995

THE TOTAL METRIFICATION OF MUSIC IN CANADA

As one of the final areas of Canadian life to undergo conversion, music must now begin its switch to the metric system. The changes will be eased in over a three-year period in various phases, the first coming in December of 1995. Here is the schedule of changes to be implemented as music in Canada goes metric:

PHASE ONE: DECEMBER 1, 1995 — Musical rhythms will change from their accustomed style to the new metric beat. For example, 4/4 time will become 104.4 kilobeats, and the old favourite waltz tempo, 3/4 time, will become 103.4 kilobeats. A handy chart will be mailed to every Canadian household for quick reference.

PHASE TWO: JULY 1, 1996 — The changes here involve the naming of the various musical instruments. This move is being hailed by many in this department as a real plus for those who have trouble remembering what instruments are called. For example, the cornet will now be known as a milihorn; the trumpet, a centihorn; the trombone, a kilihorn; and the tuba, a megahorn. As you can see, this simplifies instrument nomenclature much more than by using the old imperial instrument designations.

PHASE THREE: NOVEMBER 30, 1996 — The musical scale switches at this date to metric. The old favourite "Do Re Me" will sound a little different. The basic scale of Do Re Me Fa Sol La Ti Do will now be measured in British Thermal Units, denoting a rise in tone much like the rise in hot air. Each will be divided by ten, giving you a total scale of 80, and, in the process, make singing a great deal more precise than it has ever been before. For example, it will allow a singer, if he or she chooses, to sing six BTUs under the original tone. Along with this will be a complete revision of keys for all music, with particular reference to classical music. This will result in a total transformation of all keys into Celsius. Therefore, to listeners, Grieg's Piano Concerto in A-flat Major will instantly become Grieg's Mega Keyboard Concerto in 27 Degrees Celsius. With a little practice, you'll be able to convert, automatically, pieces such as Mozart's Flute Concerto in E-flat Major, to Mozart's Centiwind Concerto in 56 Degrees Celsius.

PHASE FOUR—FINAL STEP: AUGUST 5, 1997 — The size of orchestras will change here to metric. Orchestras will be measured, from this date, not by the number of players, but by the weight of the musicians taken on a scale just before the performance. For example, a large sixty-piece orchestra will become a Four Thousand Kilogram Band.

WEIGHTS AND MEASURES CANADA WELCOMES YOUR RESPONSES AS CANADIAN MUSIC SWITCHES TO METRIC. SEND US YOUR COMMENTS CARE OF THE DEPARTMENT OF WEIGHTS AND MEASURES, 88.7 SPARKS STREET, OTTAWA, K1A 0A2.

"Now close your eyes and imagine a magic land where even idiots can be in charge."

Great Canadian Love Stories
❧ Don Cherry ❧

Don Cherry is known to most Canadians as that no-nonsense, no-fashion-sense star of *Hockey Night in Canada*'s "Coach's Corner." What many don't know is that Don Cherry also played a part in one of the "Great Canadian Love Stories."

It was winter in Kingston, Ontario, 1950, and young Don Cherry, just barely into his teens, had very little time for thoughts of romance. Don wanted to be an NHL star, so he spent all his spare time with the other boys, playing hockey on the little frozen pond by his home.

One cold day in December, when Don and his friends arrived at the pond for their daily game, there was someone new waiting for them with skates on and hockey stick in hand. Her name was Hildegarde Horspool. She was a sturdy girl, about Don's age, but three or four inches taller, and she wanted to play hockey. Young Don was furious, and said there was no way some sissy girl was going to play hockey with them, so she could just take her stick and get off their ice. This did not sit at all well with Hildegarde, so before Don could say "drop the puck," Hildegarde gave him the hardest body check he'd ever felt. He landed flat on his back on the ice, and twenty minutes later, when he regained consciousness, Don Cherry knew he was in love.

Don and Hildegarde started going steady. They would race to the pond every day after school to play hockey together. Unlike other kids they knew, they didn't become pinned—they swapped mouth guards. Hildegarde loved Don's dipsy doodle moves around the crease, and Don loved the way Hildegarde always went in the corners. But nothing made Don love Hildegarde more than those special moments when Hildegarde would drop the gloves and they'd go a couple of rounds one on one. This was his kind of girl.

Everything was perfect until one dark and icy day in February when Don arrived at the pond. Hildegarde had bad news—she was moving with her family to Japan, where she would train to become the first female sumo wrestler. Young Don was devastated. As their teary eyes met and their lips began to quiver, Hildegarde gave Don a swift hip check, and threw him to the ground. In a frenzy of unbridled passion that started at 4:03 and ended at 17:32, she planted a hickey on Don's neck so he would have something to remember her by. And then she was gone.

Because of Hildegarde's amazing strength, the love bite became permanent. It resembled a regulation CCM puck. Some say that if you look close enough, you can actually see the letters NHL in the middle of it. And that is why, to this day, Don Cherry wears unusually high shirt collars so he can hide Hilde's tricky hockey hickey.

The end.

INTERCABINET MEMO

To: Jean Chrétien
From: Paul Martin 🐾
Date: Oct. 17/95

Jean,

   Well, I've spent a lot of time looking at this GST thing and I think I've finally found something that will replace it. It took a great deal of research on my part. I even had to take an extra algebra class at night school to get the math right. It was worth it, though, because I now have the formula for the perfect replacement to the GST, as follows:

   Take original GST @ 7% - 7% + 1995 x years to next election + total of revenue neutral incoming tax - latest Angus Reid poll x e=mc2 +/- .04% x 3lbs bananas + 27,000,000 pop. - (x5-y+8=xy) x eeny meeny miney mo = 6 to 1 / 1/2 doz. to other x the fixed hypotenuse of the angle of the dangle - 1 potato 2 potato 3 potato 4 + 1 c. flour, sifted - 2 x 3 + 4 - 1 + $.25 gets a cup of coffee +/- 12% PST = 89% GST

   I'm sure you'll agree that this will solve our GST problems. As a matter of fact, I feel confident that once this is implemented, we'll never have to worry about the GST again. Gosh! I don't know why I didn't think of it sooner.

   See you in the House,

Paul

🐾 For the last budget, Finance Minister Paul Martin did all the calculations on his toes, which explains his three-year deficit reduction theory.

"You mean dey name dose Dr. Martens after you?"

The Bloc still leads 53-52 as Manning goes for the extra point.

CBC news technicians use state-of-the-art machinery to decipher Rex Murphy's commentary.

THE MOVIE MATCH GAME

Match the entries from Column A with the movies from Column B

Column A	Column B
Pierre Trudeau	*The Big Sleep*
Brian Mulroney	*The Fisher King*
The Reichmans	*The Untouchables*
Preston Manning	*Indecent Proposal*
The Tories	*Big*
Kim Campbell	*The Good, the Bad and the Ugly*
The Canadian Senate	*The Last Emperor*
Wallace McCain	*And Then There Were None*
The PEI Fixed Link	*Brief Encounter*
Brian Tobin	*The Unforgiven*
The Canadian debt	*Brother from Another Planet*
MP pensions	*Reversal of Fortune*
The Quebec Referendum	*How the West Was Won*
RSP, UIC, and GST	*A Bridge Too Far*

Preston Manning can cross all his toes, as one crosses one's fingers for luck, which is something he has done many times while thinking about becoming prime minister.

"Boom Boom" Walker, Canada's first door-to-door bomb salesman.

"Yeah, but if I wear my helmet backwards like dis,
de enemy will tink I'm retreating."

A POLITICAL JOKE

Here is a Canadian political joke to tell at parties and really impress your friends, not only with your razor-sharp knowledge of Canadian politics, but also your skill at telling jokes. This joke is best told using the two voices of the participants, or a reasonable facsimile. At Double Exposure corporate headquarters in Vancouver this would be fairly easy, considering that both Linda and Bob are professional mimics. However, we can offer you expert tips for the presentation of this joke. When doing the voice of Jacques Parizeau, if you do not already have an ample stomach to rest hors-d'oeuvres plates on, stick a pillow in your shirt. As well, remember that he speaks with a British accent combined with a breathy Gallic mumble, highlighted by great pauses and frequent "Ahhs" or "Umms" that sound a lot like a cow that badly requires milking. When finishing the joke with the Chrétien punch-line, screw your mouth over to the right side of your face and speak with a Quebecois accent while doing a Fat Albert (Hey! Hey! Hey!). Follow these instructions and you will receive thunderous applause spotted with howls of laughter.

Premier Jacques Parizeau bumps into Prime Minister Jean Chrétien on the streets of Montreal. Parizeau immediately says, "By Jove, Chrétien, you seem to be ignoring us! Let me tell you again exactly what it is the Pequistes want. We want sovereignty, and sovereignty means that we have our own unique country, unlike anywhere else in Canada. We speak just one language. We have our own special culture. We use the same money, and sit in the same parliament as you, but you do not dare tell us what taxes to have or how to run our government. That is sovereignty!" Chrétien looks Parizeau right in the eye and says, "Hey! Dat's not sovereignty. Dat's Alberta!"

Canadian turbot quota after the EU agreement.

CUSTOMS / IMMIGRATION CANADA

Customs / Immigration Officer

The successful candidates will either have no friends or a certificate proving they cannot get along with others. They must be either naturally surly, or at least prepared to put aside normal good manners in favour of a fulfilling career. The ideal candidates will enjoy all aspects of a thorough but silent search of a family car, finding secret delight in frightening kindergarten-age passengers, huddling, nearby, out of the rain. Those lucky few chosen for this highly regarded profession will salivate at the thought of inspecting shipments of books for pornographic material. This secretly erotic exercise will go beyond mere photos of willies and bums, and into the netherworld of printed pornography. The ability to read and comprehend beyond a Grade Ten level will not hinder our successful candidates. The climax to this hunt for dirt will be professionally satisfying. Finally, our chosen candidates will feel perfectly at ease in ill-fitting, dowdy uniforms, reminiscent of Hitler's military bands. All applicants for the job of Canada Customs/Immigration Officer should be neither male nor female, but a scowly hybrid of the worst of both sexes.

APPLY TO:
Canada Customs and Immigration / Hiring Division
Attn: H. Himmler
Bunker 462
Ottawa, Ontario
K1A 0A2

THE DOUBLE EXPOSURE CANADIAN HISTORY

1. **One of Pierre Trudeau's most famous quotations was:**
   (a) "Just watch me!"
   (b) "Has anyone got a watch?"
   (c) "I'd prefer to watch."

2. **The Fenian Raids of 1866 were carried out by:**
   (a) troops from Fenia
   (b) protesters from *Fenian's Rainbow*
   (c) rebel hand puppets led by Casey and Fenian

3. **Laura Secord tricked the American soldiers by:**
   (a) leading her cow across enemy lines
   (b) having a cow
   (c) opening a Cow's Ice Cream store

4. **Mackenzie King once said:**
   (a) "Conscription if necessary, but not necessarily conscription."
   (b) "Prescription if necessary, but not necessarily prescription."
   (c) "So I subscribe to *Chatelaine*. Wanna make something out of it?"

5. **"Coureurs de bois" means:**
   (a) runners of the woods
   (b) having the runs in the woods
   (c) bicycle delivery of lumber

6. **BNA stands for:**
   (a) British North America Act
   (b) Bad Night in Alberta
   (c) a genetic test for British genes

7. **Complete this expression, "The Mounties always get their_____:"**
   (a) man
   (b) knickers in a knot
   (c) donuts from Tim Hortons

8. **When Alexander Mackenzie reached the Pacific, he wrote these words on a rock:**
   (a) Alexander Mackenzie, from Canada by land
   (b) Al loves Fanny
   (c) Grad 1765

9. **Marconi was famous for:**
   - (a) the first transatlantic wireless signal
   - (b) inventing Kraft Dinner
   - (c) eating Kraft Dinner

10. **In 1897, men were lured to the Yukon by:**
   - (a) gold
   - (b) clean rooms and cable TV
   - (c) 100 free Air Miles

11. **Billy Bishop is best remembered as:**
   - (a) a great fighter pilot
   - (b) a really wacky clergyman
   - (c) Captain Highliner's little friend

12. **The Diefenbunker** 🧦 **was:**
   - (a) a nuclear bomb shelter
   - (b) a distant cousin of Archie Bunker
   - (c) a bed that slept two prime ministers

13. **General Wolfe's role at the Plains of Abraham was:**
   - (a) the winner
   - (b) back-up goalie
   - (c) T-shirt concessions

14. **The Last Spike was:**
   - (a) the final connector in the transcontinental railway
   - (b) what Brian Mulroney inserted into Joe Clark's back
   - (c) the title of Spike Jones' last album

15. **In 1778, Captain Cook turned up on:**
   - (a) the Pacific Northwest coast
   - (b) a bed of lettuce with tartar sauce
   - (c) the Dini Petty Show

16. **The Hudson's Bay Company was most famous for:**
   - (a) fur trading
   - (b) Scratch and Save Sales
   - (c) Cher commercials

17. **The Family Compact is best described as:**
   - (a) a minority that controlled government
   - (b) all the fun of a minivan at half the price
   - (c) a household garbage crusher

18. **Sir Sanford Fleming was famous for naming:**
   - (a) time zones
   - (b) mucous in the back of the throat
   - (c) a TV show starring his son and himself

19. **Louis Riel was the only one who knew:**
   - (a) what the Metis wanted
   - (b) all the words to "Louie Louie"
   - (c) how they get the caramel in Caramilk

20. **In 1949, the people of Newfoundland began:**
   - (a) life as Canadian citizens
   - (b) collecting UI
   - (c) complaining about the Spanish

🧦 After a wild night of carousing in his early days in Parliament, John Diefenbaker had a picture of a beaver tattooed on his right big toe, explaining why he was never seen without his shoes and socks during his time as prime minister.

"Hey, look! There goes Mulroney walking his dog. Let's jump him!"

First Canadian diagnosed with *Streptafuzzacocolis* —
chest hair growing through the collar.

the skip
a squat man
squats down
hacking
in the hack
great, steaming,
hacking breath
the stub of a cigarette
three inches of ash
dangling
dangling
from the corner of his mouth
the ash falls
his ass rises
pushes, slides, throws
whoppa, whoppa
whoppa, whoppa
whoppa, whoppa
whoppa, whoppa
"No!"
slides
"Yes! Yes!"
whoppa, whoppa
whoppa, whoppa
whoppa, whoppa
"No!"
bokk, bokk
whoppa, whoppa

CURLING MEMORIES

"And after about two forkfuls, I threw up on this Japanese guy sitting way over there."

JAG BHADURIA'S MP's Report

Greetings, Dear Constituent:

It has certainly been a busy few months for your hard-working Member of Parliament. For those of you who have not been watching the Parliamentary Channel, let me first of all bring you up to date on my work in the House of Commons. I was very successful in passing my private member's Bill C-3PO, which now makes it legal to carry a loaded cruise missile in your pants. This is another victory in my fight for the right of the common Canadian to bear warheads. Once I had unanimous consent on Bill C-3PO, I then drafted a highly complex solution to the Quebec sovereignty problem. I will not bother you now with all the brilliant details, but let me just say it involves large quantities of Prozac, the Montreal Canadiens, some remote islands off the coast of Madagascar, and Ginette Reno. The prime minister was so impressed that he put my plan into effect immediately.

Since I last reported to you, I have added a Ph.D. to my credentials. I am now Jag Bhaduria, Doctor of Sub-atomic Molecular Excavation, and when I'm not in Question Period, I am building a radioactive microparticle fusion extender and cappuccino maker in my office, for which I was just awarded the Nobel Prize for interesting appliances.

But let me assure you, I have not spent all my time solving the country's problems on Parliament Hill. I have also been busy in my lovely riding (even though it is hard to get away when the president of the United States keeps calling me asking for my advice on how to handle the Republicans in Congress. Well, I just tell him the same thing I always tell the Pope, just do what you want to do, and if they give you grief, tell them you're going to go get yourself the biggest tank you can find, and you'll drive right over their heads and then back up and do it again until . . . well, I'm getting off the topic). So anyway, back in my wonderful riding of Markham-Whitchurch-Stouffville, I have been spending a great deal of my time listening to the concerns of my constituents, and as always, they won't let me go until I heal a few lepers and make the lame walk. It seems an MP's work is never done. Plus on one particular day, I spent hours in a bus that was going over 90 kph, because it had a bomb attached to it that would explode if we went below 80 kph. I had to find a way to defuse the bomb, without injuring any of my constituents or the lovely young actress driving the bus. Of course, my training as an undercover CSIS agent came in handy in defusing the bomb, which I did. Immediately following I married the lovely young actress, and then I took everyone on a nice tour of my riding. And wouldn't you know it, those evil demons, the Ontario Provincial Police, pulled me over and gave me a speeding ticket for travelling 50 kph over the speed limit. I told them some of my passengers had to get home to watch me on the Parliamentary Channel. They weren't impressed by that, so then I told them they'd better stand back, because I had an armed cruise missile in my pants, which, I reminded them, was now legal. The officers were obviously unaware of my private member's bill, because suddenly they started calling for back-up. Anyway, to make a long story a little longer, I can tell you, as your MP, I will fight this speeding ticket with every ounce of strength that I have, and then I will go and find that tank, because my name is Jag Bhaduria, which is Hindi for "I drive British cars very, very fast!"

Well, I must close off now, as the prime minister has an appointment with me. No doubt he will beg me once again to come back to the Liberals. He does this practically every week. Last time he offered me both Sheila Copps' and Paul Martin's portfolios. Of course, I turned him down. Believe me, dear constituent, I accomplish much more for you, as an independent MP, without some boss man breathing down your neck, checking every little detail, telling you all the time, "you can't say that," or "is that really true?" I mean, whatever happened to democracy? And so, dear constituent, until next time, remember my motto:

"Vote for Jag Bhaduria and get the MP you deserve."

Here my close personal friend Bob Robertson, of *Double Exposure*, accompanies me on the piano during my recent singing debut on Rita MacNeil's TV show.

Here I am posing with my close personal friends Lloyd Axworthy and Herb Gray, just before attending the Parliament Hill Halloween party.

Here I am posing with the Port Hawksbury Rifle and Rug Battalion after I awarded many of their members the coveted Jag Bhaduria Medal of Bravery for their tireless work in retrieving toupees lost in heavy winds, particularly mine.

Here I am posing with the president of the EU after I single-handedly solved the turbot crisis.

Bye for now,

jAg

Sir John A. Macdonald calmly attempts the Heimlich manoeuvre on himself after choking on a chicken bone.

For All Time

How do Canadians remember their leaders?
Like any other country, we name things after them.
Here's a list of some of our leaders
and how they live on in posterity.

Who: Frederick Arthur Stanley, sixth governor general of Canada
What was named after him:
  Stanley Park, Vancouver
  The NHL's Stanley Cup
Most recognized for: The Stanley Garage Door Opener
Background: Lord Stanley was a well-known amateur inventor during his stay in Canada, and the now-famous garage door opener was installed by Lord Stanley himself in the carriage houses of most Ottawa dignitaries during the 1880s. He was also player/coach for the first professional hockey team in Canada, which, because of its dreadful play, was named the Stanley Tools. Its legacy is carried on today by the Ottawa Senators hockey team.

Who: Sir John A. Macdonald, first prime minister of Canada
What was named after him:
  Macdonald-Cartier Freeway
  Macdonald's Export "A" cigarettes (little-known fact: the Fathers of Confederation asked him to smoke outside during the Charlottetown Conference of 1864)
Most recognized for: Macdonald's restaurants
Background: Although better known for his drinking habits, Sir John, in fact, was a

voracious eater. His annual summer barbecue on Parliament Hill turned into the capital's first drive-through, with Sir John himself cooking some of his Scottish fast-food favourites, like the Haggis Quarter Pounder, or the Big Hag, and Filet of Hag. Children were treated to such promotions as Fathers of Confederation Action Figures. His famous golden arches sign with the words "Tens Served" became a legend across Upper Canada.

Who: Sir Mackenzie Bowell, fifth prime minister of Canada
What was named after him:
  The Bowell Haircut (copied later by the Three Stooges)
  The Bowell Movement (nickname for his election campaign)
Most recognized for: The vessel we now know simply as "The Bowl"
Background: The bowl was invented by Prime Minister Bowell in conjunction with his Conservative successor, Sir Charles Tupper. Together, they began calling at the homes of fellow members of parliament to demonstrate their handy plastic storage containers, and Tupperware was born.

Who: Mackenzie King, tenth prime minister of Canada
What was named after him:
  King Street, Toronto
  King Clancy (Toronto hockey player and coach)
Most recognized for: *King of Kensington* (Canadian TV series)
Background: Although the cathode ray tube was still in the experimental stages when King became prime minister in 1921, the idea of it fascinated him. In later years he would speak to the spirit of his dead mother, and through those conversations, the pilot script for *King of Kensington* was fleshed out. The last piece of the puzzle fell into place after many hours of King's dead mother yelling "Wax! Wax!" After spending the whole day shining the floors of his house, it finally occurred to King that his mother meant Al Waxman, the legendary Canadian star of this long-running TV series.

Who: Joe Clark, sixteenth prime minister of Canada

What was named after him:

  Clark Drive (major traffic route in Vancouver)

  Adrienne Clarkson (Indian princess who later married Clark's son)

Most recognized for: The High River, Alberta, sewage treatment system

Background: Although the town of High River, Alberta, had already named a school after Joe Clark, many citizens felt that was not enough. When the new sewage treatment system was opened, city fathers recognized their opportunity to pay Joe Clark back for his many months of service as prime minister, and named the new sewage treatment system the "What a Waste Plant."

Who: John Napier Turner, seventeenth prime minister of Canada ("Old Slap and Tickle")

What was named after him:

People who make up jokes, laugh and then slap someone on the backside are said to have a "Napier wit."

Best recognized for: Tina Turner, rock singer.

Background: After witnessing John Turner carry out Pierre Trudeau's patronage appointments, Tina was overheard to say, "I want to have his child, or, barring that, I'll take his name."

Who: Brian Mulroney, eighteenth prime minister of Canada

What was named after him:
The *Oxford English Dictionary* says his name is now
recognized as the only eight-letter swear word in the English language.

Anything else: Not so far.

"Excuse me, Prime Minister, what does this mean, '*most* of Canada'?"

"Alright, alright, I'll leave B.C., just don't shoot!"

— Hockey's FIRST Sex Change —

BERT/BETTY "FIVE HOLE" MAKITA

Ol' "Five Hole," as he was known when he played left wing on the famous "Big Tools" line (Bert Makita, Johnny Black, and Andre Decker), was a real marksman in the slot, and probably one of the toughest hitters in the entire game. After a Stanley Cup victory one year, his team, the New York Fries, toured Sweden. Following the first exhibition game against the Gotenberg Saunas, Bert stayed behind in the dressing room while his teammates headed for a Swedish drinking establishment, the Blonde Bimbo Bar and Grill. Bert promised to meet them there. Later that night, a stranger in Gotenberg and completely lost, he finally rang the bell at the Blonde Bimbo Sex Change Shop, just off Hardiegardie Street. In a drunken stupor, he allowed the owner, Anders Anderson, to switch his sex from male to female. By the time her fellow players found her, Betty had already married a Swedish logger named Ulfie Ulferson. Until she was brought down heavily by a bodycheck against the Boston Bruins in the early '30s, Betty Makita remained one of the most feared players in the game, because not only could she still hit like a ton of bricks, she could now cut you down to size with a few well-chosen words. Betty Makita, the NHL's first two-way player.

Betty "Five Hole" Makita

HOLY SKOKE

Memo

To: All Liberal caucus members

From: Roseanne Skoke, Lib. Halifax

My fellow Liberals, as you are all no doubt aware by now, I am the heavenly conscience of the Liberal Party of Canada, and I want to alert you, once more, to the fact that all homosexuals are bad. They are bad because the Bible says so. They are unnatural. But even worse than that, they are bad because they are conspiring to destroy the heterosexual world. How? Let me enlighten you. First, they have completely taken over the hairdressing industry, so when we heterosexuals go for a cut and blow dry, they intentionally give us ridiculous styles, simply to humiliate us. Well, look at my hair: ridiculous! I went to the parliamentary salon. I thought I was perfectly safe. My stylist's name was Rocky. I mean, who knew? He had all those muscles rippling through his T-shirt and really, really tight pants, so tight you could almost see his, well, anyway, this is the haircut I end up with. And they tell you "Oh, this is the latest style!" Well, I haven't seen one other person with this stupid style. They also control the clothing industry and design bizarre clothes that we heterosexuals are forced to wear, resulting, once again, in our humiliation. In the meantime, while we poor, unsuspecting heterosexuals are preoccupied with trying to do something decent with this ridiculous hair, and these idiotic clothes, they steal our big German shepherds and collies and Labradors, and replace them with poodles and Yorkshire terriers and those terrible chihuahuas. A God-fearing heterosexual wouldn't be caught dead with one of those bald, bug-eyed barking rats. And as the takeover becomes complete, they're going to force us to go to Broadway musicals, and call each other "darling," and we'll start saying "please" and "thank you" a lot, and they'll make us decorate our homes with complementary colours, and we'll start drinking cappuccinos, and excercising to Richard Simmons, and they'll make Toller Cranston the prime minister! And I say to you today, that I will fight to my very last breath to make sure that Canada is safe from this kind of pure evil.

Thank you, and God bless

P.S. See you in chapel at 10:30 for "Prayers to Guide Us Safely Through Question Period."

Excited Innu receives his first two-dollar coin.

THE DOUBLE EXPOSURE SPORTS

1. **Performance-enhancing steroids are:**
   (a) the reason Ben Johnson lost his gold medal
   (b) a lozenge for sore throats
   (c) what the federal Tories could use right
       about now

2. **If you won the Queen's Plate, you would have won:**
   (a) the premier Canadian horse race
   (b) Queen Elizabeth's dentures
   (c) the daily lunch special at the Ontario
       legislature cafeteria

3. **The greatest scoring moment in Canadians' memories is:**
   (a) Paul Henderson's famous goal
   (b) Margaret Trudeau and The Rolling Stones
   (c) the Winnipeg Jets taxpayer bailout

4. **A Threepeat means:**
   (a) champion three years in a row
   (b) Peter Pocklington, Peter Mansbridge
       and Peter Newman on TV at the same time
   (c) three Quebecers sharing a beachside condo in
       St. Petersburg

5. **Curling is Canada's favourite winter sport because:**
   (a) Canada has a lot of ice
   (b) the drive-in theatres are closed
   (c) no one squats or sweeps like a Canadian

6. **The original Canadian sport, invented by natives, is:**
   (a) lacrosse
   (b) the wild buffalo-milking contest
   (c) casino gambling

7. **You would find Silken Laumann in:**
   (a) a single scull
   (b) a Benadril TV commercial
   (c) the lingerie department, right next
       to the panty girdles

8. **If someone introduced you to Eddie Shack, you would:**
   (a) meet a weird old hockey player in a suitcase
   (b) be in a building where matches are stored
   (c) discover Shaquille O'Neal's first name

9. **Don Cherry is married to:**
   (a) a woman named Rose
   (b) a dog named Blue
   (c) Doug Gilmour

10. **When Canadians hear the name Jackie Parker, they think of:**
    (a) one of the CFL's greatest players
    (b) John F. Kennedy's wife
    (c) a parking attendant named Jackie

Russian play-by-play crew for World Hockey Championships.

11. **When you hear high-powered cars roaring through city streets, it's:**
    (a) the Molson Indy
    (b) Yonge Street on a Saturday night
    (c) people heading for "20% off Rubbermaid Days" at Canadian Tire

12. **Show jumping is something that:**
    (a) Big Ben is famous for
    (b) Pamela Wallin is famous for
    (c) what they do on the All-bungee Channel

13. **Canada's figure skating champion is:**
    (a) Elvis Stojko
    (b) Elvis Costello
    (c) always high on McCain's Fruit Punch

14. **Canada has produced many skeet shooting champions because:**
    (a) we have a skeet shooting tradition
    (b) the skeet hunting season runs year 'round
    (c) with our winters, Canadians learn to skeet at an early age

15. **In the NHL, the Lady Byng Trophy goes to:**
    (a) the most gentlemanly player
    (b) the most attractive cross-dresser
    (c) the player's wife who most sounds like Bing Crosby

16. **The most popular sport at the Big O is:**
    (a) watching the Expos topple the opposition
    (b) watching the concrete topple from the walls
    (c) watching Quebecers hunt for the architect

17. **Canada has two football teams named "The Roughriders" because:**
    (a) no one knows
    (b) we got a two-for-one deal from Acme Football Names
    (c) we're idiots

18. **Canada's most famous downhill team was:**
    (a) the Crazy Canucks
    (b) the Lazy Gourmets
    (c) Kim Campbell's Tories

19. **The phrase "Gee Willikers!" was spoken by:**
    (a) Howie Meeker after a great play
    (b) Paul Martin, when he saw the size of Canada's debt
    (c) viewers watching Howie Meeker's commercial for the 31st time

20. **The Vancouver Millionaires is what you would call:**
    (a) the Stanley Cup winners from 1912
    (b) most of the players on the Canucks
    (c) the only people who can afford to buy a house there

Although Sharon Carstairs was famous for having Canada's tiniest voice, few people were aware that she also had Canada's largest feet: size 47 1/2 DDD. Consequently, she was the gold medalist in the Barefoot Waterskiing event at the 1963 Summer Olympics in Reykjavik, Iceland.

A happy fan rushes to meet Jean Chrétien, as he beats other world leaders
in the gruelling G-7 Bicycle Marathon.

"Now turn him around and let me see Lucien Bouchard."

"I bring you a message from John Crosby. He says his hearing has returned." ⅊

⅊ After one particularly loud argument in the Parliamentary cafeteria, John Crosby was forced to drink tequila from Sheila Copps' Reeboks.

From Parliament

PRIVATE MEMBERS' BILLS THAT WERE NEVER PASSED

Member: Mort Passton (Ref.)
Riding: Calgary-Stetson
Bill C-654–"Cadaver Immigration"

Whereas: current immigration rules allow all sorts of rabble into this country, mostly foreigners, and whereas this rabble does nothing but add to the welfare rolls, start up gangs that rob people, and steal thousands of minimum-wage jobs away from Canadians, and whereas it has been proven that they all lie and claim that Fidel Castro would send his German shepherds after them if they were sent back home to China; and whereas it is obvious that there is not one living one of them fit to become a Canadian; be it resolved that the Immigration Board allow only non-living immigrants into Canada, and change the name of said board to "The Cadaver Processing Board," realizing that cadavers rarely, if ever, work for minimum wage, start gangs, or go on welfare, and also be it resolved that cadavers entering Canada with ten thousand dollars or more continue to be fast-tracked into the system, with the full realization that the funeral home industry of Canada would benefit greatly, requiring thousands to be hired to properly dispose of these immigrant cadavers, bringing down unemployment figures and becoming the engine that will drive the greatest economic growth in this century, we hereby recommend passage of this Bill C-674–"Cadaver Immigration."

Technicians from *The National* measure light reflection from Peter Mansbridge's head.

Great Canadian Love Stories
✥ Mr. Dressup ✥

For more than two decades, children all over Canada have grown up with Mr. Dressup, his little pal Casey and their pet dog Finnegan. But how many remember that Mr. Dressup was also the leading man in one of the "Great Canadian Love Stories"?

In the early days, Mr. Dressup, Casey and Finnegan were happy together. Casey would spend his time playing in the tree house out back, Finnegan would bury bones all over the yard, and Mr. Dressup would teach all the kids who tuned in every day lots of useful things, like how to make sweaters out of a sheet of construction paper, a ball of string and two empty egg cartons, plus the many fun and practical ways to use parsnips.

Then one day, there was a knock at the door. When Mr. Dressup opened it, he couldn't believe his eyes. Standing before him was the most beautiful woman he'd ever seen. She wore a starched white uniform, with shiny white work shoes, and floating around her was the alluring fragrance of Pine Sol. Her name was Miss Clean and Shiny, and she'd just moved into the time slot right after Mr. Dressup. She was going to teach all the little boys and girls the wondrous joys of good personal hygiene. Mr. Dressup instantly fell in love with Miss Clean and Shiny, and she with him. They had a whirlwind courtship and were married the next day by Captain Billy, an old friend from Mr. Dressup's earlier unsuccessful kids' show *Mr. Dressup and the Captain Gut Fish*. So Miss Clean and Shiny became Mrs. Dressup and they had a lovely honeymoon—in Canada's Wonderland, of course.

Casey and Finnegan loved Mrs. Dressup. They would all play Ring Around A Rosie together, and Finnegan would bark with glee. Mr. and Mrs. Dressup couldn't be happier. They spent day after contented day decorating their little house, making all their furniture and appliances out of empty toilet paper rolls, balls of aluminium foil and paper clips. Who could have foreseen what would happen next? One day, while Mr. Dressup was in the backyard, teaching Casey how to make a Boeing 737 out of a Kleenex box, three avocado pits and jam, someone came to the front door.

When Mr. Dressup and Casey came in to tell Mrs. Dressup about their successful test flight, the house was empty. Mrs. Dressup was gone! All they found was a note that read, "Mr. Dressup, I'm leaving you for the Friendly Giant. I just had to, because he has a special chair waiting just for me. P.S. If only you'd worn those tights. P.P.S. Always remember, Q-tips are our friends. Yours sincerely, Ms. Clean and Shiny-Dressup-Giant." That was the last they ever saw of Mrs. Dressup. It was such a blow to them all that from that day on, Casey didn't grow another inch and Finnegan never barked again. As a matter of fact, Casey went through a very difficult period. He started to act out, his language got quite bad, and he refused to work with the hand that was up his shirt. He was arrested on more than one occasion for racing through the *Take Thirty* set and flashing Adrienne Clarkson. Casey is now in a twelve-step program for recovering puppets. And Mr. Dressup has spent the last nineteen years building a nuclear power plant out of toothpicks, old dish soap bottles and elastic bands, just to erase the memory of one of the "Great Canadian Love Stories."

The end.

"I can get rid of hospitals and I can get rid of schools,
so why can't I get rid of this damn constipation!?"

Land claims negotiator Irving Feldman.

CORPS OF COMMISSIONAIRES

Professional Commisssionaires

The successful candidates will have proudly served, and been reluctantly discharged as drill sergeants in any branch of Canada's armed forces, although ex-Airborne Regiment members will be given priority consideration over other candidates. These former screaming boot camp supervisors will feel perfectly at home directing traffic and giving out tickets at Canada's busiest airports, knowing that pedestrians blocking crosswalks with luggage will respond to them as happily as zit-faced goons assembling rifle parts. Ideal candidates for the Corps will be able to proudly address vehicle owners as "Arseholes" in both official languages. Many of our successful candidates will go beyond traffic control to determine whether ordinary citizens are fit to pass into the elevators at hundreds of Canada's tallest buildings. A lack of knowledge as to which businesses occupy the building will not hinder our candidates from many years of service at the "front doors of industry." The cheery slogan, "Look at the bloody sign!" will fall from our candidates' lips as easily as their ample stomachs will hang over the belts of their standard-issue trousers. Finally, our chosen candidates, despite rigorous physical and verbal tickling, will not crack a smile under pressure. They will also display no sense of humour whatsoever, remembering that this is what finally defeated the Axis Powers during our candidates' glory years in the '40s.

APPLY TO:
Corpses of Commissionaires, War Museum, Ottawa KIA oA2

"And then I thought, 'Heck! Why not fly **under** the Lions Gate Bridge!'"

IN MY HEADSET

Welcome to Air Canada's "Concert in the Clouds" . . .

Captain again. Those clouds are blocking our view of Wawa . . .

Mesdames et messieurs, le capitaine . . .

Is Luciano Pavarotti, accompanied by . . .

Something from the bar before dinner . . .

Which will be presented on original instruments . . .

Like a Heineken or a glass of . . .

Beethoven's Fifth, which rises to . . .

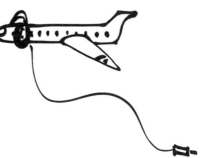

Lower your window shades for the film . . .

Which was written in 1734 by . . .

***Forrest Gump.* The English is on channel . . .**

Forty-seven concertos for orchestra by his . . .

Mother always said, Life is like a . . .

Chicken teriyaki or steak, sir? With the steak you . . .

Never know what you're gonna get . . .

Looks like we've got some turbulence . . .

Which would last my whole life, giving me . . .

Thirty-eight thousand feet for the rest of our trip . . .

Over mother's bedroom, where men would have . . .

Hot rolls with your meal? Or how about some . . .

Crooked legs which just felt like . . .

Curry over your chicken, then you'll . . .

Run, Forrest, run!!!

"And if you don't let us become the official opposition, I'll begin shooting myself every hour until the plane is empty!"

In a rare shot, a photographer captures the excitement
of feeding time in the Tory compound.

In their search for the Southwest Passage, crew members of the first ship to attempt sailing across the southern prairies show surprise as they cruise into Regina Harbour.

Excerpts from
THE CANADIAN DRIVER'S GUIDE

Winter Driving in Canada

Winter driving in Canada can be hazardous, and the best way we know of to prepare you properly is to be trained by a resident of the prairie provinces. These are the only Canadians who actually know how to drive in snow. In fact, they are so skilled at driving in snow, they go out even when they don't have to, just for the sheer joy of showing off their skills at handling their vehicles in less-than-ideal conditions. The ultimate thrill for them comes when the RCMP issue warnings to drivers to "stay off the highways unless absolutely necessary." You can count on prairie drivers to leap into their cars at this moment and show the world how really well they can drive in snow. We highly recommend calling someone you know who lives on the prairies and asking them to teach you how to drive. This applies especially to Vancouver or Victoria drivers who become petrified at the first sign of light snow falling (some do not even know what the white flakes are called), and book the day off work. We are not sure, but suspect that an atmospheric phenomenon connected to the heavy magnetic qualities of the Canadian Shield makes any driver who lives west of Alberta or east of Manitoba a whimpering bundle of fear when attempting to drive in snow. Once again, we repeat: have someone from the prairies teach you how to drive in snow. Only they know how.

Four-way Flashers

The Great Driving Secret
Police Will Never Tell You About

All vehicles, by law, must come equipped with four-way flashers. However, most Canadians have no idea how useful these devices can be. They will allow you to park in all tow-away zones, handicapped and commercial parking spots, bus stops, and even no-stopping lanes on busy streets. How do they work? Simple. By leaving your vehicle parked in any of these illegal stopping areas with the four-way flashers in operation, this signals to police, ticket issuers, tow truck drivers and the rest of the population that you are "only stopping for a minute." This makes you totally immune to receiving tickets or being towed. Probably only about 5 percent of Canadian drivers are aware of what their four-way flashers can do for them. No more driving 'round and 'round the block searching for a parking spot. No more scrambling for change for parking meters. All because of that little button on your steering column. Court records show, time and time again, that cases have been thrown out when drivers can prove they had their four-way flashers on. Don't bother asking the police. They will never tell one of the best-kept secrets in the highway traffic code: four-way flashers.

"Damn! Must have been a seagull from Ontario!"

OTTAWA TREK
— THE NEXT GENERATION —

(The teenagers of the '90s become the parliamentarians of the future.)

* * *

HOUSE OF COMMONS

Monday, May 8, 2025

The Speaker (Ms. Wilson): The dude from Calgary Southwest.

Mr. Jason Mann (Calgary Southwest, Ref.): Cool. So, like is this a joke or something, or, like is the minister for real about the deficit or what, man?

Some hon. members: Yo! Yo!

The Speaker (Ms. Wilson): The honourable dude, the Minister of Finance.

Hon. Dana Wong (Minister of Finance, Lib.): Cool. So, I'm like listening to this no-brain right, and I'm like yeah, right, sure. I mean . . . Earth to dude!! Earth to dude!! The deficit is big, man! Get it?

Some hon. members: Awesome dude! Radical!

The Speaker (Ms. Wilson): The babe from Beaches–Woodbine.

Ms. Kirstin Fletcher (Beaches–Woodbine, Cons.): Cool. Like my question is for the Minister of Fisheries? Hello?? Hello?? Like she said all the fish had disappeared? And I'm like, give me a break, eh?

Some hon. members: Brilliant! Get real!

The Speaker (Ms. Wilson): The honourable babe, the Minister of Fisheries and Oceans.

Hon. Dee Dee Devray (Minister of Fisheries and Oceans, Lib.): Cool. Like, so maybe they might come back, eh? Like, it could happen!

Some hon. members: Totally rad, man! Far out!

The Speaker (Ms. Wilson): Like, time is up for Question Period. Are you with me, dudes and dudettes?

Some hon. members: Cool! Cool!

"You know, with this zoom lens, I can almost see the Tories across the House!"

"There's a woman trapped in her bedroom!"
"Well, it's another job for the little fireman."

"See! I told you whining gets you into cabinet!"

THE CANADIAN GOLFER

I awake with the first rays of sunshine,
My excitement I cannot contain,
For today I know victory will be mine,
My power I will not restrain.

I arrive at the club bang on eight,
Custom-made Spaldings in tow,
I've got all the gadgets that ever were made—
Oh I use them, they're not just for show!

Golf shoes Gucci, shorts Golden Bear,
I am Mulligan, God of the Drive!
To win at this game, no expense I will spare—
To chip is to know you're alive.

It's tee-off time and I'm first to go,
I'm bustin' to show them my stuff.
I've bought all the books, hired the pro—
Ha! I laugh in the face of the rough.

My heart surges like a freshly charged golf cart,
Visions of eagles dance in my head.
Eyes down, pull back, rip that ball apart,
Then, the sound, the sound that I dread:

Whack *#!@ Whack *#!@ Whack *#!@ Whack *#!@
Ahh, there's something wrong with my club!
Whack *#!@ Whack *#!@ Whack *#!@ Whack *#!@
The ball soars two feet and lands in a shrub!

Whack *#!@ Whack *#!@ Whack *#!@ Whack *#!@
Who the hell planted that tree there!
Whack *#!@ Whack *#!@ Whack *#!@ Whack *#!@
Excuse me, ma'am, gotta play my ball in your hair.

Whack Splash *#!@ Whack Splash *#!@ Whack Splash *#!@
What's the deal with all this water?
Whack Splash *#!@ Whack Splash *#!@ Whack Splash *#!@
Damn it, Jim! I'm a golfer, not a friggin' otter!

Whack *#!@ Whack *#!@ Whack *#!@ Whack *#!@
Eighteen lousy holes I chased that useless ball,
Whack *#!@ Whack *#!@ Whack *#!@ Whack *#!@
Whose idea was this *#!@ game after all?

Whack *#!@ Whack *#!@ Whack *#!@ Whack *#!@
Score? 147. I'm filled with shame and sorrow,
Whack *#!@ Whack *#!@ Whack *#!@ Whack *#!@
God! I can't wait till I come back tomorrow.

Quebec waits while nature calls.

INDEX

Newman, Don, newscaster and jazz singer, 483

Nowhere. *See* Direction of Federal NDP, 328

Oral hygienists, new jobs for Airborne Regiment soldiers, 440

Pequistes, or Pequistos, spraying with Raid works, 348

Quebec, province, "Still Crazy After All These Years," 107

Robertson, Lloyd, new hair colour choices on view, 218

Saskatchewan, province, "Who's Who of Who's left," 388

Summer, season in Canada, very brief summary, 891

Toronto, city, nice place to be from, 670

Uklavit, capital of Iklavut, NWT, 456

Victoria, city, God's Waiting Room revisited, 996

Winnipeg, the PST, GST and JST (Jets Sales Tax), 170

Yellowsnow, from Joni Mitchell song, "Don't Eat It!", 233

Zalm, nickname for "The Zalmer of B.C.," local tulip farmer, 401 👣

Throughout his political career, Bill Vander Zalm suffered from severe "Foot in Mouth" disease. After many tests and consultations, doctors concluded that the only cure was to either have his feet removed, or his mouth sewn shut. Mr. Vander Zalm chose the former.

Linda Cullen

It has been a well-kept secret that Linda Cullen is actually the first-ever test-tube baby. There is no documentation of this fact in the official medical history books, mainly because the ground-breaking procedure was not performed in a hospital or clinic with a petrie dish. Instead, Linda's parents decided to do it at home, using an old Shake'n Bake bag, which is why to this day she still picks up frozen chickens in the grocery store and yells "Mommy?"

She attended Henry Birks Senior Secondary, and, like most other teens, went through a rebellious period. She joined an unruly gang called "The Latex," which would break into houses and paint the interior with really bold colours. People weren't so much terrified as annoyed, because they had to keep recovering their furniture.

Following high school, Linda went to college and graduated *Mazda cum slo lae* as a fully certified Flag Person. She soon rose to the top of her profession, and became famous for using the "Slow" sign in situations where historically the "Stop" sign had been used exclusively. But even though she had attained this unparalleled success, deep down inside she knew there was something else she wanted to do. A voice had been calling to her that she could no longer ignore, and she finally realized what she really wanted—to be a green pepper! However, as a vegetable, she realized she would be limited to work in politics or sportscasting, and therefore chose comedy instead.

Bob Robertson

Bob Robertson grew up in Ajax, Ontario, just east of Toronto. Ajax, of course, is well known internationally as the home of the world's only Ajax mine, the original and, so far, only source of the foaming cleanser. Ajax, like its cousin Borax, has been a much-used cleanser for thousands of years. It is reported that Indians living along the shores of Lake Ontario discovered the large Ajax deposits before the arrival of explorers like Cartier. They used it to clean their canoes after long journeys. The element Ajax, or, by its atomic weight, A_2FC, that is, two parts Ajax, to one Foaming Cleanser, is mined in the heart of the town of Ajax by thousands of the town's citizens. It is estimated that there is a large enough supply of the element to last until the year 3000, if used as directed.

It was in this atmosphere that Bob Robertson grew up, played with the children of miners, and attended Ajax High School. He was an average student, but excelled at basketball, playing for the much-feared Ajax Abrasives. He also was a regular performer with the Ajax High School Drama Club, famous for training the soap opera stars of today. His broadcasting career took him across Canada on a route similar to that of Alexander Mackenzie, but without a canoe. He now resides in Vancouver, where he rarely misses his home town, except on the occasional trip past the household cleanser shelves of his local supermarket. Does he actually use Ajax in his home? Does it snow in Kapuskasing?

Photograph Credits